Happy Hippo.

Water.

Splash!
Happy Hippo is in the water.

Down.

Up.

Eddy Elephant is not in the water.

Happy Hippo is in the water.

Splash!
Eddy Elephant is in the water.

Eddy Elephant splashes
Happy Hippo.

Happy Hippo splashes the water.

Down.

Up.

Eddy Elephant is not in the water!